The Black Death

Sarah Blackmore

Published in association with
The Basic Skills Agency

Hodder Murray

A MEMBER OF THE HODDER HEADLINE GROUP

Photo acknowledgements
p.7 Physician, 1790 © Medical-on-line/Alamy; p.17 Self-punishment woodcut © akg-images; p.25 The Great Fire of London, 1666 © akg-images.

Hodder Headline's policy is to use papers that are natural, renewable and recyclable products and made from wood grown in sustainable forests. The logging and manufacturing processes are expected to conform to the environmental regulations of the country of origin.

Orders: please contact Bookpoint Ltd, 130 Milton Park, Abingdon, Oxon OX14 4SB. Telephone: (44) 01235 827720. Fax: (44) 01235 400454. Lines are open from 9.00am to 5.00pm, Monday to Saturday, with a 24-hour message answering service. Visit our website at www.hoddereducation.co.uk

© 1999 NTC/Contemporary Publishing Group 1999, 2000, 2006
Adapted for the Livewire series in 2000 by Sarah Blackmore
First published in the Livewire series in 2000 and first published in the Hodder Reading Project series in 2006 by Hodder Murray, an imprint of Hodder Education, a member of the Hodder Headline Group, an Hachette Livre UK Company, 338 Euston Road, London NW1 3BH

Impression number   10 9 8 7 6 5
Year   2011 2010 2009 2008 2007

Cover photo: Carving on wall of plague ossuary © Nicole Duplaix/Corbis.
Internal artwork © Oxford Designers and Illustrators.
Typeset by SX Composing DTP, Rayleigh, Essex.
Printed in Great Britain by CPI Bath.

A catalogue record for this title is available from the British Library

ISBN-13: 978 0 340 91573 8

Contents

1
Bring Out Your Dead!

Bring out your dead!
Bring out your dead!

That was the cry
heard all over Europe in the 1300s.
It was the cry of the cart drivers as they
drove their carts between the houses,
picking up dead bodies.
The carts were filled with corpses.
Sometimes they were piled high.

Bodies were dragged from almost every house
and thrown on to the carts.
Body was tossed on top of body.
There were piles of dead bodies,
like logs in a pile of wood.

The drivers looked for doors
on which a cross had been painted.
These were the houses
where someone in the family
had the plague.
Sometimes two or three bodies
would be dragged from the same house.
The Black Death had struck.
The plague!

The Black Death killed
most of the people who got it.
In fact,
it killed millions of people across Europe.

In one large Russian city,
only five people survived the plague.
In London,
nine out of every ten people died of it.
In some countries almost everybody died.

It was not long before there were
no coffins left.
Dead bodies were thrown on top of each other.
They were piled high in huge pits,
then a thin layer of dirt was thrown over them.

2
No Escape

The plague spread very quickly
from person to person.
People went to bed well,
but the next day they were dead.

A doctor might try to treat somebody
with the plague,
but then the doctor would catch it as well.
The doctor died with the patient,
and sometimes even before.

Some doctors tried to protect themselves.
They wore a type of mask.
It looked like a large beak.
The beak was filled with things
that had a strong smell –
things like vinegar or sweet oils.
This stopped the doctors from smelling
dead or dying people.

Doctor wearing a protective mask

They even used a rod
to take the patient's temperature because
they did not want to touch them.

People tried to get away from the plague.
They tried to get away from each other.
Husbands left wives.
Parents left children.
Many people tried to leave
the towns and cities.
They thought that they would be safe
in the country.
They were wrong.
There was no escape from the plague.

3
Why the 'Black' Death?

The plague meant death,
but why was it called the 'Black' Death?

Let's imagine that you have the plague.
First you find lumps.
There may be lumps under your arms
or in your groin.
These lumps are the size of eggs.
You will have a bad cough,
a really bad cough.
You will sweat a lot.
Added to this you will have black patches
all over your skin.
You will be dead in three days.

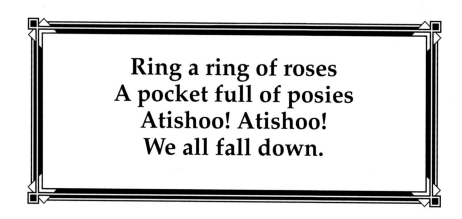

**Ring a ring of roses
A pocket full of posies
Atishoo! Atishoo!
We all fall down.**

This children's song is about the plague.

Ring a ring of roses
The first sign of the plague was lumps.
They were spots or blisters
with rings around them.
They were rose coloured.

A pocket full of posies
Some people carried a posy of flowers
in their pocket.
They thought it would protect them.
It also helped to get rid of the smell
of people dying.

Atishoo! Atishoo!
One of the last symptoms of the plague
was sneezing.

We all fall down
After sneezing, people died.

4
How Did it Spread?

So where did the plague come from?
Where did it start?

It started in China,
and it spread very quickly
through lots of countries.
It came to Great Britain in 1348.

How did the plague spread?
We know that it spread
from person to person.
When people moved from one country to another,
they took it with them.

The spread of the plague

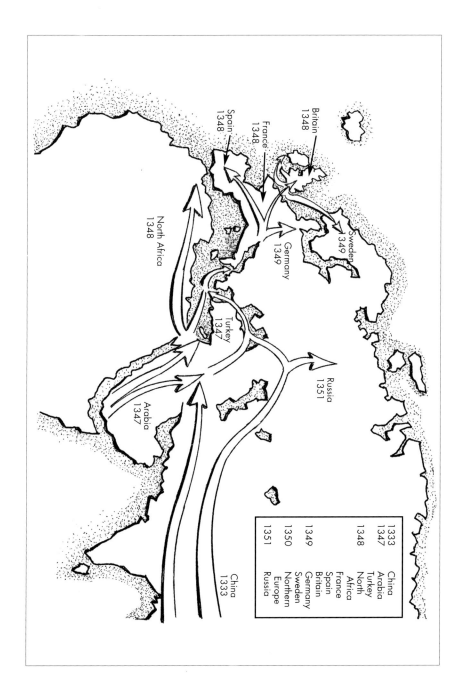

Britain 1348

Spain 1348

France 1348

North Africa 1348

Sweden 1349

Germany 1349

Turkey 1347

Arabia 1347

Russia 1351

China 1333

1333	China
1347	Arabia
1348	Turkey
	North
	Africa
1349	France
	Spain
1350	Britain
	Germany
1351	Sweden
	Northern
	Europe
	Russia

An army of people called the Tartars
fought across Europe.
They took the plague with them.

One story tells of how the Tartars
used dead bodies as weapons.
They used the bodies of those
who had died of the plague.

They had always used huge catapults
to throw stones against walls.
They did this to fight their way
into towns and cities.

But at one city the Tartars did not use stones.
They loaded the catapults with dead bodies,
and threw them over the city walls.

The people in the city
were terrified that they would catch the plague.
Many ran away,
taking the plague with them.

The Black Death spread quickly.
It killed so many people,
in so many countries.
No one understood how it travelled.
It was frightening.

5
An Act of God?

Some people thought that the plague
had been sent by God as a punishment.
They thought that God must be
very angry with them.
They got together in groups,
and tried to punish themselves
for making God angry.

They dressed in sackcloth and ashes.
They beat themselves with whips
made of leather.
The whips had metal tips on the end.
By doing this they hoped that God
would stop the Black Death.

Self-punishment: some people thought this might make God stop the Black Death

People were so scared of the plague,
it made them think and do all sorts of things.
Nobody knew how the plague had started,
and nobody knew if there was a cure.
People panicked.

As time went on, food began to run out.
The people who farmed the land
were all dying.
There was no one left to tend the crops.
Fields were full of dead animals.

People wondered if and when it would end.
They thought it was the end of the world.

6
The Cause

So what did cause the plague?
Lots of ideas were put forward.

One idea was that there were cracks
in the Earth.
People thought that the cracks were caused
by planets passing too close to Earth.
They thought that gas
was escaping from the cracks,
and that the gas was poison
which caused the plague.

People did not know what had caused
the plague.
Because they did not know the cause,
they could not work out a cure.
They did all sorts of crazy things.

They tried anything to get rid of
the Black Death.
Some ate lizards and toads.
Some drank blood and other disgusting things.
Some ripped open
the bodies of puppies and birds.
They held them against the boils on their bodies.

What did cause the Black Death?
Something had to carry the plague germs.
Something did.
Rats!

Or, to be accurate,
it was carried by the fleas on rats.
The fleas lived on the rats,
and they drank their blood.
The plague germ lived in the fleas.

The fleas then jumped on to people.
Flea bites spread the plague in humans.

7
An End to the Plague

The plague went on and on.
This Black Death lasted for about 200 years,
then it died away.

Some people think that the plague was
stopped by fire.
The Great Fire of London in 1666
did mark the end of the plague in London,
because it killed most of the rats
and the fleas with them.

The Great Fire of London, 1666

For 200 years the Black Death
killed many millions of people
all over Europe,
and it was only one of many plagues
that swept across the continent.

It was caused by flea bites
and was passed from person to person.
A disease that can be passed on in this way
is called contagious.

If only people had known more about germs
back in 1300!
Today we know how important it is
to keep things clean.
Keeping things clean
protects us from some germs.
Soap and water could have helped
to protect people from the Black Death,
if only they'd known.

Today the plagues of the past
can be cured by antibiotics
and by keeping places clean.